Puree Cookbook for Adults

A Family-Friendly Nourishing and Delicious Puree Recipes for People with Swallowing and Chewing Difficulties

Antonio Colon

Table of contents

Introduction

In the heart of a bustling city, where the aroma of spices danced through the air and the clatter of pots and pans filled the streets, there was a humble little restaurant "The Puree Haven." It was a land of gastronomic magic, where tastes mixed, textures altered, and ordinary ingredients transcended into spectacular concoctions.

At the head of this culinary refuge was Chef Antonio, a maestro of pureeing, whose enthusiasm for the art of blending had no boundaries. With a sparkle in his eyes and a whisk in his hand, he worked his magic in the kitchen, making pureed marvels that thrilled even the most discriminating palates.

Customers would flock to "The Puree Haven," not just for a meal, but for an experience—a symphony of taste that unfolded with every spoonful. Chef Antonio's purees were like potions, weaving together the essence of materials, infusing them with his passion for food and his steadfast devotion to culinary excellence.

Inspired by the enchantment that unfurled in his restaurant, Chef Antonio started on a mission to share the wonder of pureeing with the world. And so, the "Puree Cookbook for Adults" cookbook was born—a testament to the transformative power of pureeing.

Within the pages of this amazing cookbook, you will go on a gastronomic trip like no other. Each recipe has been thoughtfully developed to highlight the magic of blending, where basic components are lifted to astonishing heights. From smooth soups and velvety sauces to delicious desserts and inventive side dishes, Chef Antonio's creations will take you on a voyage into a world where tastes merge seamlessly and textures tickle the senses.

But this cookbook is more than simply a compilation of recipes—it is an invitation to embrace your inner alchemist, explore the boundless possibilities of pureeing, and uncover your own culinary magic. Through thorough directions, professional recommendations, and compelling tales, "Puree Cookbook" will enable you to uncover the hidden potential of your foods and unleash your creativity in the kitchen.

Whether you are an aspiring chef, a home cook aiming to enrich your dishes, or an adventurous food lover seeking new experiences, "Puree Cookbook for Adults" will be your guide to unlocking the mysteries of blending and releasing the hidden powers of pureeing. Step into the world of Chef Antonio and let his enthusiasm fire your culinary creativity.

Did you know that pureed food is blended food that can be eaten with a spoon, has a smooth texture, and requires nearly no chewing? A pureed diet might help you receive enough food when you are having difficulties chewing or swallowing.

In addition to maintaining proper oral intake, pureed meals may even lower the chance of choking.

Added bonus: pureed meals for adults are simple to create!

This book delves into the specifics of pureed food for adults, including how to make your own, where to get pre-made pureed meals, and some basic pureed food recipes.

Why Do You Need Pureed Food?

Pureed meals are a form of texture alteration that aids with issues connected to chewing and swallowing. A pureed diet consists of meals that are mixed, whipped, or mashed until they reach a "pudding-like" texture.

Pureed Food for Swallowing Problems

For persons with swallowing challenges, ensuring sure the meal has the proper consistency is vital. Pureed foods for swallowing difficulties include pureed fruits and vegetables, milkshakes, desserts, and soups.

A speech therapist (or speech-language pathologist) is typically engaged with giving suggestions for texture alteration recommendations. A certified dietician is concerned with providing nutrition education and supporting the preparation of healthy meals.

If you are experiencing difficulties swallowing meals, then you should speak to your doctor. Certain tests may be necessary to detect swallowing difficulties like dysphagia, and other health concerns, and to make sure you're eating the proper texture of foods.

Pureed Food for Chewing Problems

A pureed diet may be advantageous for those who are missing teeth, are experiencing mouth discomfort, or are recovering from a dental procedure. Pureed food assists those with chewing issues because these meals need no chewing.

In addition to pureed meals, there are soft foods that don't need chewing for people with chewing difficulty.

High-calorie beverages are especially good for persons who cannot or have problems chewing, or who have difficulty swallowing meals.

So, open the pages of "Puree Cookbook for Adults" and immerse yourself in a domain where tastes are altered, where textures are exalted, and where simple ingredients become magnificent works of art. Prepare to be charmed by the magic of pureeing and let your kitchen become a stage for culinary enchantment.

Chapter 1: The Basics of Pureeing

Understanding Purees

Purees are smooth, creamy, and typically thick culinary dishes produced by blending or processing components into a soft and homogenous texture. They are typically linked with infant food, although they are as nutritious and delightful for adults.

Purees offer a simple method to digest healthy meals, particularly for persons with swallowing difficulty, dental concerns, or those who prefer smoother textures. They may be produced from a broad range of components, including vegetables, fruits, legumes, meats, grains, and more.

The process of pureeing entails breaking down the components into a constant, homogeneous texture, which makes them simpler to swallow and digest. The final purée is smooth, without any lumps or solid bits.

This texture alteration may be performed by numerous means, such as utilizing blenders, food processors, immersion blenders, or specialist pureeing equipment.

Benefits of Purees for Adults

Purees provide various advantages for adults, beyond only convenience and simplicity of ingestion. Here are some benefits of including purees in the adult diet:

Improved Digestion: Purees give a smoother consistency that needs less chewing and decreases the stress on the digestive system. This may be especially advantageous for those with digestive issues, such as gastroesophageal reflux disease (GERD) or irritable bowel syndrome (IBS).

Swallowing problems: Some medical disorders or operations might result in swallowing problems, known as dysphagia. Purees are an ideal alternative for those with dysphagia since they minimize the need for prolonged chewing and make swallowing safer and more controllable.

Increased Nutrient Intake: Purees allow for the incorporation of a broad variety of foods, guaranteeing a diversified range of nutrients in each meal. By mixing fruits, vegetables, proteins, and grains together, you can make delectable and nutrient-rich purees that provide a balance of vitamins, minerals, fiber, and antioxidants.

Weight control: Purees may be a beneficial aid in weight control or weight reduction programs. By managing portion sizes and using whole, unprocessed foods, purees may help people attain and maintain a healthy weight while still enjoying great meals.

Versatility and Variety: Purees provide unlimited opportunities for culinary innovation. You may experiment with various taste combinations, textures, and spices to create a fascinating and diverse meal. Additionally, purees may be used as a basis for other meals or as an ingredient in recipes such as soups, sauces, and baked goods.

Tools and Equipment for Pureeing

To generate smooth and uniform purees, having the correct tools and equipment is vital. Here are some regularly used products for pureeing:

Blender: A high-quality blender is a flexible tool for pureeing. Look for blenders with robust motors, sharp blades, and different speed settings to handle varied ingredients and textures. Countertop blenders are often more powerful, whereas immersion blenders give the convenience of mixing directly in the pot or container.

Food Processor: Food processors are good for processing bigger amounts of materials and generating a rougher or smoother texture, depending on the desired output. They are especially helpful for turning solid meals into purees, such as vegetables, lentils, or cooked meats.

Immersion Blender: Also known as a hand blender or stick blender, an immersion blender is a small and handy piece of equipment for pureeing. It comprises a portable motor with a mixing wand that may be plunged straight into a pot or container. Immersion blenders are perfect for mixing hot soups or small amounts of purees.

Food Mill: A food mill is a classic instrument used for pureeing and straining cooked fruits and vegetables. It consists of a bowl with tiny holes, a grinding plate, and a handle. By twisting the handle, the components are driven through the perforations, resulting in a smooth purée.

Sieve or Strainer: A fine-mesh sieve or strainer may be used to produce a smooth and velvety texture in purees. By pressing the ingredients through the sieve using the back of a spoon or a spatula, any remaining lumps or fibers can be removed, resulting in a refined puree.

Food Dehydrator: While not essential, a food dehydrator can be a useful tool for pureeing certain ingredients. By dehydrating fruits or vegetables, you can enhance their flavor, concentrate their nutrients, and create a more intense puree.

Cutting Board and Knife: A strong chopping board and a sharp knife are necessary equipment for prepping components before pureeing. They allow for efficient and precise cutting, peeling, and slicing of fruits, vegetables, and other ingredients.

Tips for Successful Pureeing

To acquire the greatest results while pureeing, consider the following tips:

Choose Ripe and Fresh Foods: Select fresh, ripe, and high-quality foods for the best taste and nutritional value. This is especially critical when dealing with fruits and vegetables since their flavor and texture dramatically affect the final puree.

Cook or Steam Ingredients: For vegetables, legumes, and meats, it's normally suggested to heat or steam them before pureeing. This softens the components and makes them simpler to combine into a smooth consistency.

Manage the Liquid: When pureeing, it's crucial to manage the quantity of liquid used. Start with a tiny quantity and gradually add more as required to get the desired consistency. Remember that it's simpler to thin down a puree than to thicken it, so add liquid gradually.

Seasoning and Flavoring: Don't be hesitant to add herbs, spices, and seasonings to your purees. They may improve the taste and make the purees more palatable. Experiment with various combinations to discover your favorite flavor.

Texture Modifications: If you like a somewhat chunky puree, pulse the components momentarily instead of blending them constantly. This enables a textured effect with little fragments remaining. Conversely, if you desire an ultra-smooth puree, blend for a longer duration or strain it through a fine-mesh sieve.

Portion and Freeze: Purees may be produced in bigger quantities and frozen in individual amounts for later use. This saves time and ensures you always have a range of healthful alternatives readily accessible.

Apply Food Safety: Remember to apply adequate food safety procedures while handling, preparing, and storing foods. Keep utensils and equipment clean, and refrigerate or freeze purees quickly to ensure their quality and safety.

By learning the principles of pureeing, comprehending the advantages for adults, having the necessary tools and equipment, and following valuable guidelines, you can go on a path of preparing tasty and nutritious purees to enrich your culinary experiences and encourage a healthy lifestyle.

Chapter 2: Vegetables and Legumes

2.1 Classic Mashed Potatoes

Ingredients:

4 big potatoes (russet or Yukon Gold)

4 tablespoons unsalted butter

½ cup milk (whole or 2%)

Salt, to taste

Pepper, to taste

Instructions:

Peel the potatoes and chop them into uniformly sized bits. This ensures that they cook uniformly and allows for simpler mashing.

Rinse the potato pieces under cold water to eliminate extra starch.

Put the potatoes in a large pot and pour cold water over them. Add a pinch of salt to the water to season the potatoes while they boil.

Bring the saucepan to a boil over medium-high heat and then decrease the heat to a simmer. Cook the potatoes for around 15-20 minutes or until they are fork-tender. They should be soft enough to readily penetrate with a fork.

While the potatoes are boiling, simmer the milk and butter together in a small saucepan over low heat until the butter has melted. Keep the mixture heated.

Once the potatoes are done, drain them completely and return them to the saucepan. Place the saucepan back on the burner over low heat to evaporate any leftover liquid from the potatoes.

Begin mashing the potatoes with a potato masher or a fork. Mash them until they achieve the required consistency. For smoother potatoes, continue mashing until no lumps remain. For a chunkier texture, leave some little bumps.

Gradually pour the heated milk and butter mixture into the mashed potatoes, stirring gently to integrate it. Keep adding the mixture until the desired creaminess is attained. Be cautious not to overmix, since it might make the potatoes gluey.

Add salt and pepper to taste when preparing the mashed potatoes. Adjust the seasoning as required.

Transfer the mashed potatoes to a serving plate and top with a dollop of butter or chopped herbs, if preferred. Serve immediately when still hot.

Prep Time: Approximately 30 minutes

Nutritional Value (per serving):

Calories: 220, Fat: 10g, Carbohydrates: 31g, Fiber: 2g, Protein: 3g

Note: Nutritional values may vary based on the precise components and quantity utilized.

2.2 Creamy Carrot Puree

Ingredients:

1-pound carrots, peeled and sliced

2 tablespoons unsalted butter

½ cup veggie broth (or water)

¼ cup heavy cream (or milk for a milder variation)

Salt, to taste

Pepper, to taste

Fresh herbs for garnish (optional)

Instructions:

In a medium-sized pot, add the sliced carrots and cover them with vegetable broth or water. The liquid should be just enough to cover the carrots.

Using a medium-high heat, bring the liquid to a boil. Reduce the heat to a simmer and cook the carrots for approximately 15-20 minutes or until they are soft when pricked with a fork.

Once the carrots are done, drain them, saving part of the cooking liquid.

Transfer the cooked carrots to a food processor or blender. Add the butter, heavy cream (or milk), salt, and pepper.

Blend the ingredients until smooth and creamy. If required, add a tiny amount of the remaining cooking liquid to reach the desired consistency. The purée should be silky and readily spreadable.

Taste the puree and adjust the seasoning, if required, by adding additional salt and pepper according to your desire.

Transfer the silky carrot puree to a serving plate. If desired, garnish with fresh herbs such as parsley or chives to provide a burst of color and taste.

Serve the puree immediately while still warm, with your favorite main courses.

Prep Time: Approximately 30 minutes

Nutritional Value (per serving):

Calories: 150, Fat: 10g, Carbohydrates: 14g, Fiber: 4g, Protein: 2g

2.3 Silky Butternut Squash Soup

Ingredients:

1 medium-sized butternut squash, peeled, seeds, and cubed

1 tablespoon olive oil

1 medium onion, chopped

2 cloves garlic, minced

4 cups vegetable broth

½ cup heavy cream (or coconut cream for a dairy-free alternative)

1 teaspoon ground cumin

½ teaspoon ground cinnamon

Salt, to taste

Pepper, to taste

Fresh herbs or roasted pumpkin seeds for garnish (optional)

Instructions:

In a large saucepan, warm the olive oil over medium heat. Add the chopped onion and minced garlic, and sauté until the onion turns translucent and the garlic is aromatic.

Add the diced butternut squash to the saucepan and sauté for a few minutes to gently cook the squash and improve its taste.

Pour in the vegetable broth, ensuring that it covers the squash. Bring the mixture to a boil, then decrease the heat to low and let it simmer for approximately 20-25 minutes, or until the squash is fork-tender.

Once the squash is cooked, gently transfer the mixture to a blender or use an immersion blender straight in the saucepan. Blend until the soup achieves a smooth and creamy consistency.

Return the blended soup to the pot (if using a blender) and set it over low heat. Stir in the heavy cream (or coconut cream) to give richness to the soup.

Add the ground cumin and cinnamon to the saucepan, stirring carefully to blend the flavors. To taste, add salt and pepper to the food.

Simmer the soup for an extra 5 minutes to enable the flavors to melt together. Adjust the seasonings as required.

Ladle the smooth butternut squash soup into serving dishes. If preferred, garnish with fresh herbs like parsley or cilantro, or sprinkle toasted pumpkin seeds over top for extra texture and taste.

Serve the soup hot and enjoy its soothing sweetness.

Prep Time: Approximately 45 minutes

Nutritional Value (per serving):

Calories: 200, Fat: 10g, Carbohydrates: 26g, Fiber: 5g, Protein: 3g

2.4 Spicy Sweet Potato Mash

Ingredients:

2 big sweet potatoes, peeled and cubed

2 tablespoons unsalted butter

¼ cup milk (whole or 2%)

1 teaspoon ground cumin

½ teaspoon chili powder

½ teaspoon paprika

¼ teaspoon cayenne pepper (adjust to taste)

Salt, to taste

As a garnish, use fresh cilantro or green onions.

Instructions:

Place the sweet potato cubes in a big saucepan and fill them with water. Add a pinch of salt to the water to season the potatoes while they boil.

Bring the pot's temperature to a rolling boil over medium-high. Reduce the heat to a simmer and cook the sweet potatoes for approximately 15-20 minutes, or until they are soft when poked with a fork.

Once the sweet potatoes are cooked, drain them completely and return them to the saucepan.

Add the butter, milk, ground cumin, chili powder, paprika, and cayenne pepper to the saucepan with the sweet potatoes.

Using a potato masher or a fork, mash the sweet potatoes and stir in the spices and butter until thoroughly blended. Continue mashing until you obtain a smooth and creamy texture.

Taste the mash and season with salt according to your desire. As needed, adjust the spices and seasonings.

Transfer the spicy sweet potato mash to a serving dish. If desired, sprinkle with fresh cilantro or chopped green onions to give a burst of freshness.

Serve the mash immediately while still hot, with your favorite main courses.

Prep Time: Approximately 30 minutes

Nutritional Value (per serving):

Calories: 180, Fat: 6g, Carbohydrates: 30g, Fiber: 5g, Protein: 3g

2.5 Green Pea and Mint Puree

Ingredients:

2 cups frozen green peas

2 teaspoons fresh mint leaves, chopped

2 tablespoons olive oil

1 minced garlic clove, along with 1/2 teaspoon of lemon zest

1 tablespoon lemon juice

Salt, to taste

Pepper, to taste

Instructions:

Cook the frozen green peas according to the package directions. Drain them and put them aside.

In a food processor or blender, mix the cooked green peas, fresh mint leaves, olive oil, minced garlic, lemon zest, and lemon juice.

Blend the ingredients until smooth and creamy. If required, add a tiny bit of water or olive oil to reach the appropriate consistency. Although thick, the purée should be spreadable.

Taste the purée and season with salt and pepper according to your liking. Adjust the taste if required by adding extra lemon juice or mint.

Once the puree is fully combined and seasoned, transfer it to a serving basin.

If preferred, top the green pea and mint puree with a drizzle of olive oil and a few fresh mint leaves for enhanced freshness and presentation.

Serve the puree at room temperature or refrigerated, depending on your choice. It may be served as a dip with crackers or veggie sticks, or as a spread over toast or sandwiches.

Prep Time: Approximately 15 minutes

Nutritional Value (per serving):

Calories: 120, Fat: 6g, Carbohydrates: 14g, Fiber: 4g, Protein: 4g

2.6 Roasted Beetroot Puree

Ingredients:

4 medium-sized beetroots, peeled and cut

2 tablespoons olive oil

2 cloves garlic, minced

1 teaspoon balsamic vinegar

Salt, to taste Pepper, to taste

Fresh herbs for garnish (optional)

Instructions:

Preheat the oven to 400°F (200°C).

In a large mixing basin, stir the diced beetroots with olive oil, minced garlic, balsamic vinegar, salt, and pepper. Ensure that the beetroots are fully covered with the seasoning.

Spread the seasoned beetroots in a single layer on a baking sheet.

The beetroots should be roasted in the preheated oven for 30 to 40 minutes, or until they are soft to the fork and have caramelized. Stir the beetroots once or twice throughout the roasting procedure to achieve equal cooking.

Remove the roasted beetroots from the oven and allow them to cool slightly.

Transfer the roasted beetroots to a food processor or blender and pulse until smooth and creamy. If required, add a tiny bit of water or olive oil to reach the appropriate consistency.

Taste the puree and adjust the seasoning with salt and pepper according to your desire.

Once the puree is fully combined and seasoned, transfer it to a serving basin.

If preferred, top the roasted beetroot puree with fresh herbs like parsley or chives for enhanced freshness and appearance.

Serve the puree at room temperature or refrigerated, depending on your choice. It may be consumed as a dip with bread, crackers, or vegetable sticks, or as a spread over sandwiches or toast.

Prep Time: Approximately 15 minutes

Roasting Time: Approximately 30-40 minutes

Nutritional Value (per serving):

Calories: 80, Fat: 4g, Carbohydrates: 10g, Fiber: 3g, Protein: 2g

2.7 Lentil and Vegetable Soup

Ingredients:

1 cup dry lentils (green or brown), washed and drained

2 tablespoons olive oil

2 peeled and sliced carrots and 1 chopped onion

2 celery stalks, chopped

2 cloves garlic, minced

1 teaspoon ground cumin

1 teaspoon ground paprika

½ teaspoon dried thyme

4 cups vegetable broth 2 cups water

1 bay leaf Salt, to taste

Pepper, to taste

Fresh parsley for garnish (optional)

Instructions:

In a big saucepan, heat the olive oil over medium heat. Add the diced celery, carrots, and onion, all chopped. Sauté for approximately 5 minutes, or until the veggies begin to soften.

Add the minced garlic, ground cumin, ground paprika, and dried thyme to the saucepan. Stir well to coat the veggies with the spices and heat for a further minute until aromatic.

Add the washed lentils to the saucepan and toss to mix them with the veggies and spices.

Pour in the veggie broth and water. Salt and pepper the dish after adding the bay leaf.

Bring the soup to a boil, then decrease the heat to low. Cover the saucepan and simmer for approximately 25-30 minutes, or until the lentils are soft and the flavors have melted together.

Once the lentils are cooked, taste the soup and adjust the seasoning with salt and pepper if required.

Remove the bay leaf from the soup.

Ladle the lentil and vegetable soup into serving dishes. If preferred, garnish with fresh parsley for a blast of freshness and extra flavor.

Serve the soup hot and enjoy its warming and nutritious properties.

Prep Time: Approximately 15 minutes

Cooking Time: Approximately 30 minutes

Nutritional Value (per serving):

Calories: 250, Fat: 6g. Carbohydrates: 40g, Fiber: 12g, Protein: 12g

3.1 Creamy Chicken and Vegetable Puree

Ingredients:

1 boneless, skinless chicken breast

1 tablespoon olive oil

1 onion, chopped

2 carrots, peeled and sliced

2 celery stalks, chopped

2 cloves garlic, minced

4 cups chicken broth

2 cups chopped potatoes

1 cup frozen peas

1 cup chopped broccoli florets

½ cup heavy cream (or coconut cream for a dairy-free alternative)

Salt, to taste

Pepper, to taste

Fresh parsley for garnish (optional)

Instructions:

In a big saucepan, heat the olive oil over medium heat. Add the minced garlic, diced celery, carrots, and sliced onion. Sauté for approximately 5 minutes, or until the veggies begin to soften.

Add the boneless chicken breast to the saucepan and heat until it is browned on both sides.

Pour in the chicken broth, ensuring that it covers the chicken and veggies. Bring the mixture to a boil, then decrease the heat to low and let it simmer for approximately 15-20 minutes, or until the chicken is cooked through and the veggies are soft.

Once the chicken is done, take it from the saucepan and leave it aside to cool somewhat. Shred the chicken using two forks.

Return the shredded chicken to the pot. Add the diced potatoes, frozen peas, and chopped broccoli florets. Stir well to mix.

Continue cooking the mixture for a further 10-15 minutes, or until the potatoes are cooked.

After removing the saucepan from the heat, let the mixture to slowly cool.

Transfer the mixture to a blender or use an immersion blender right in the saucepan. Blend until the soup achieves a smooth and creamy consistency.

Return the blended soup to the pot (if using a blender) and set it over low heat. Stir in the heavy cream (or coconut cream) to give richness to the purée.

Season the creamy chicken and vegetable purée with salt and pepper to taste. Adjust the seasonings as required.

Simmer the puree for an extra 5 minutes to enable the flavors to mingle together.

Ladle the creamy chicken and vegetable purée into serving dishes. If desired, sprinkle with fresh parsley for extra freshness and appearance.

Serve the puree hot and enjoy its warming and nutritious characteristics.

Prep Time: Approximately 15 minutes

Cooking Time: Approximately 45 minutes

Nutritional Value (per serving):

Calories: 350, Fat: 15g, Carbohydrates: 25g, Fiber: 4g, Protein: 28g

3.2 Tender Beef Stew Puree

Ingredients:

1-pound beef stew meat, chopped into tiny cubes

2 tablespoons olive oil

1 onion, chopped

2 carrots, peeled and sliced

2 celery stalks, chopped

2 cloves garlic, minced

2 cups beef broth

1 cup diced potatoes

1 cup chopped tomatoes (canned or fresh)

1 cup chopped mushrooms

1 teaspoon dried thyme

1 bay leaf Salt, to taste

Pepper, to taste

Fresh parsley for garnish (optional)

Instructions:

In a big saucepan, heat the olive oil over medium heat. Add the minced garlic, diced celery, carrots, and sliced onion. Sauté for approximately 5 minutes, or until the veggies begin to soften.

Add the beef stew meat to the saucepan and heat until it is browned on both sides.

Pour in the beef stock, ensuring that it covers the meat and veggies. Add the diced potatoes, diced tomatoes, chopped mushrooms, dry thyme, and bay leaf to the saucepan. Stir well to mix.

Bring the mixture to a boil, then decrease the heat to low and let it simmer, covered, for roughly 1.5 to 2 hours, or until the beef is soft and the flavors have blended.

Once the beef stew has been done, remove the bay leaf from the saucepan.

Allow the stew to cool somewhat before transferring it to a blender or using an immersion blender right in the saucepan. Blend the ingredients until it achieves a smooth and creamy consistency. If required, add a tiny quantity of water or beef broth to modify the thickness of the puree.

Return the purée to the saucepan (if using a blender) and set it over low heat. Stir vigorously to cook the purée thoroughly.

Season the soft beef stew purée with salt and pepper to taste. Adjust the seasonings as required.

Simmer the puree for a further 5 minutes to ensure it is cooked evenly.

Ladle the purée into serving dishes. If desired, sprinkle with fresh parsley for extra freshness and appearance.

Serve the soft beef stew puree hot and taste its warming and nutritious properties.

Prep Time: Approximately 20 minutes

Cooking Time: Approximately 2.5 to 3 hours

Nutritional Value (per serving):

Calories: 320, Fat: 15g, Carbohydrates: 20g, Fiber: 4g, Protein: 25g

3.3 Salmon and Dill Puree

Ingredients:

8 ounces fresh salmon fillet, skin removed

1 tablespoon olive oil

1 shallot, minced

2 cloves garlic, minced

1 tablespoon chopped fresh dill

½ cup vegetable broth

Juice of ½ lemon

Salt, to taste

Pepper, to taste

Instructions:

Preheat the oven to 375°F (190°C).

Place the salmon fillet on a baking pan lined with parchment paper. Drizzle the fillet with olive oil and season it with salt and pepper.

Bake the salmon in the preheated oven for about 15-20 minutes, or until it is cooked through and flakes readily with a fork. The salmon should be taken out of the oven and given some time to cool.

Olive oil should be heated in a small pan over a medium heat. Add the minced shallot and minced garlic. Sauté for approximately 2-3 minutes, or until they turn transparent and aromatic.

Add the veggie broth to the pot and bring it to a boil. Cook for a further 2-3 minutes to absorb the flavors.

Transfer the cooked salmon, sautéed shallot and garlic, and the vegetable broth to a blender or food processor. Add the chopped fresh dill and lemon juice.

Blend the ingredients until it achieves a smooth and creamy consistency. If required, add a tiny quantity of water or vegetable broth to get the appropriate thickness.

Taste the puree and adjust the seasoning with salt and pepper according to your desire.

Once the puree is fully combined and seasoned, transfer it to a serving basin.

Serve the salmon and dill purée at room temperature or refrigerated. It may be eaten as a spread over crackers, bread, or vegetable sticks, or used as a delicious complement to salads or sandwiches.

Prep Time: Approximately 10 minutes

Cooking Time: Approximately 15-20 minutes

Nutritional Value (per serving):

Calories: 200, Fat: 12g, Carbohydrates: 2g, Fiber: 0g, Protein: 20g

3.4 Tofu and Spinach Puree

Ingredients:

14 ounces firm tofu, drained and pressed

2 cups fresh spinach leaves

2 tablespoons olive oil

2 cloves garlic, minced

1 tablespoon lemon juice

½ teaspoon salt ¼ teaspoon black pepper

Instructions:

Place the drained and pressed tofu in a blender or food processor.

In a pan, warm the olive oil over medium heat. Add the minced garlic and sauté for approximately 1-2 minutes, or until it turns aromatic and faintly browned.

Add the fresh spinach leaves to the pan and simmer until they wilt down approximately 2-3 minutes. After taking the pan off the heat, let the spinach cool a little.

Transfer the cooked spinach and sautéed garlic to the blender or food processor with the tofu.

Add the lemon juice, salt, and black pepper to the blender.

Blend the ingredients until it becomes smooth and creamy. If required, add a tiny bit of water to alter the consistency to your desire.

Taste the purée and adjust the spices if required.

Once the puree achieves a suitable consistency and taste, transfer it to a serving basin.

Serve the tofu and spinach purée at room temperature or refrigerated. It may be eaten as a dip for veggies, a spread on toast or crackers, or used as a creamy sauce for pasta or grains.

Prep Time: Approximately 10 minutes

Cooking Time: Approximately 5 minutes

Nutritional Value (per serving):

Calories: 150, Fat: 10g, Carbohydrates: 6g, Fiber: 2g, Protein: 12g

3.5 Turkey and Sweet Potato Mash

Ingredients:

1-pound ground turkey

2 tablespoons olive oil

1 onion, chopped 2 cloves garlic, minced 2 medium-sized sweet potatoes, peeled and diced

1 cup chicken broth ½ cup unsweetened almond milk (or your choice of milk)

1 teaspoon dried thyme

½ teaspoon ground cinnamon

Salt, to taste

Pepper, to taste

Fresh parsley for garnish (optional)

Instructions:

A big pan should be filled with heated olive oil and placed over medium heat. Add the diced onion and minced garlic. Sauté for approximately 2-3 minutes, or until they turn aromatic and transparent.

Add the ground turkey to the pan and heat until it is browned and cooked through, breaking it up into little pieces as it cooks.

Meanwhile, in a separate pot, bring water to a boil and add the diced sweet potatoes. Cook for about 10-15 minutes, or until the sweet potatoes are soft when probed with a fork. Drain the sweet potatoes and leave aside.

Once the turkey is done, drain any extra grease from the pan if required.

Add the cooked sweet potatoes to the pan with the turkey. Chicken broth and unsweetened almond milk should be added.

Sprinkle the dried thyme and ground cinnamon over the mixture. Add salt and pepper to the meal as desired.

Using a potato masher or fork, mash the turkey and sweet potato combination until it achieves a smooth and creamy consistency. Alternatively, add the ingredients to a blender or food processor and blend until smooth.

Return the purée to the skillet (if using a blender) and set it over low heat. Stir vigorously to cook the purée thoroughly.

Taste the turkey and sweet potato mash and adjust the spice if required.

Simmer the puree for a further 5 minutes to ensure it is cooked evenly.

Ladle the turkey and sweet potato mash into serving dishes. If desired, sprinkle with fresh parsley for extra freshness and appearance.

Serve the puree hot and enjoy its warming and nutritious characteristics.

Prep Time: Approximately 15 minutes

Cooking Time: Approximately 30 minutes

Nutritional Value (per serving):

Calories: 280, Fat: 12g, Carbohydrates: 20g, Fiber: 4g, Protein: 24g

3.6 Lentil and Chicken Curry Puree

Ingredients:

1 cup red lentils

1 tablespoon olive oil

1 onion, chopped 2 cloves garlic, minced 1-inch piece of fresh ginger, grated

1-pound boneless, skinless chicken breasts, chopped into tiny pieces

2 teaspoons curry powder

1 teaspoon ground cumin

1 teaspoon ground coriander

½ teaspoon turmeric powder

¼ teaspoon cayenne pepper (optional, for heat)

2 cups chicken broth

1 cup coconut milk

Salt, to taste

Fresh cilantro for garnish (optional)

Instructions:

Red lentils should be well cleaned in cold water until the water is clear. Set aside.

A large saucepan should be placed over medium heat to warm the olive oil. The chopped onion should be added and sautéed for two to three minutes, or until transparent.

Add the minced garlic and grated ginger to the saucepan. Sauté for a further minute or until aromatic.

Add the chicken pieces to the saucepan and heat until they are browned on both sides.

In a small bowl, add the curry powder, ground cumin, ground coriander, turmeric powder, and cayenne pepper (if using). Mix thoroughly to produce a spice mix.

Sprinkle the spice combination over the chicken and onion mixture in the saucepan. Stir to coat the ingredients evenly.

Add the red lentils to the saucepan, followed by the chicken broth and coconut milk. Stir well to mix.

Reduce the heat to low after the mixture has reached a boil. Cover the saucepan and let it boil for around 20-25 minutes, or until the lentils are soft and the flavors have melted together.

Once the lentils are done, remove the saucepan from the heat and allow the mixture to cool slightly.

Transfer the lentil and chicken curry mixture to a blender or use an immersion blender right in the saucepan. Blend the ingredients until it achieves a smooth and creamy consistency. If required, add a tiny quantity of water or broth to modify the thickness of the puree.

Return the purée to the saucepan (if using a blender) and set it over low heat. Stir vigorously to cook the purée thoroughly.

suit the lentil and chicken curry puree and season with salt to suit.

Simmer the puree for a further 5 minutes to ensure it is cooked evenly.

Ladle the purée into serving dishes. If desired, garnish with fresh cilantro for extra freshness and presentation.

Serve the lentil and chicken curry puree hot, and relish its fragrant aromas and nutritional characteristics.

Prep Time: Approximately 15 minutes

Cooking Time: Approximately 35 minutes

Nutritional Value (per serving):

Calories: 380, Fat: 14g, Carbohydrates: 35g, Fiber: 12g, Protein: 28g

3.7 Quinoa with Black Bean Puree

Ingredients:

1 cup cooked quinoa

one can (15 ounces) of rinsed and strained black beans

2 tablespoons olive oil

1 onion, chopped

2 cloves garlic, minced

1 teaspoon ground cumin

½ teaspoon paprika

¼ teaspoon chili powder (optional, for heat)

Salt, to taste

Fresh cilantro for garnish (optional)

Lime wedges for serving (optional)

Instructions:

In a big pan, warm the olive oil over medium heat. Add the chopped onion and sauté for approximately 2-3 minutes, or until it turns translucent.

Add the minced garlic to the pan and sauté for an additional minute until fragrant.

Add the cooked quinoa to the pan and stir well to incorporate with the onion and garlic combination.

To the skillet, add the black beans that have been washed and drained. Stir to blend with the quinoa mixture.

Sprinkle the ground cumin, paprika, and chili powder (if using) over the quinoa and black bean mixture. Stir well to thoroughly distribute the seasonings.

Season with salt to taste, altering the quantity according to your desire.

Cook the mixture over medium-low heat for about 5-7 minutes, stirring regularly, to enable the flavors to melt together.

Once the puree has cooked through and the flavors have mixed, remove the pan from the heat.

Using an immersion blender or transferring the mixture to a blender or food processor, puree the quinoa and black bean combination until it achieves a smooth and creamy consistency. If required, add a tiny quantity of water or vegetable broth to modify the thickness of the puree.

Return the purée to the skillet (if using a blender) and set it over low heat. Stir vigorously to cook the purée thoroughly.

Taste the quinoa and black bean puree and adjust the spice if required.

Simmer the puree for a further 5 minutes to ensure it is cooked evenly.

Ladle the purée into serving dishes. If desired, garnish with fresh cilantro for extra freshness and presentation.

Serve the quinoa and black bean puree hot, complemented with lime wedges if preferred, and enjoy its pleasant texture and healthy properties.

Prep Time: Approximately 10 minutes

Cooking Time: Approximately 15 minutes

Nutritional Value (per serving):

Calories: 250, Fat: 8g, Carbohydrates: 36g, Fiber: 10g, Protein: 10g

Chapter 4: Grain-Based Purees

4.1 Creamy Rice and Cauliflower Puree

Ingredients:

1 cup jasmine rice

One small head of cauliflower, chopped into florets

2 cups vegetable broth

One cup of almond milk without sugar (or another milk of your choice)

2 tablespoons butter (or dairy-free butter replacement)

2 cloves garlic, minced ¼ teaspoon ground nutmeg

Salt, to taste

Pepper, to taste

Fresh parsley for garnish (optional)

Instructions:

Jasmine rice should be well rinsed in cold water until the water is clear. Set aside.

In a large saucepan, heat the vegetable broth until it boils. Add the cauliflower florets and simmer for about 8-10 minutes, or until the cauliflower is soft when probed with a fork. Remove the cauliflower florets from the saucepan and put aside.

Butter should be melted over medium heat in the same pan. Add the minced garlic and sauté for approximately a minute until fragrant.

Add the washed jasmine rice to the saucepan and swirl well to coat it with the butter and garlic mixture.

Pour in the unsweetened almond milk and return the cooked cauliflower florets to the saucepan.

Sprinkle the ground nutmeg over the mixture. As desired, season the meal with salt and pepper.

Stir the ingredients thoroughly, then decrease the heat to low. Cover the saucepan and let the mixture simmer for about 15-20 minutes, or until the rice is cooked and has absorbed most of the liquid.

Once the rice is done, remove the saucepan from the heat and allow the mixture to cool slightly.

Transfer the rice and cauliflower mixture to a blender or use an immersion blender straight into the saucepan. Blend the ingredients until it achieves a smooth and creamy consistency. If required, add a tiny quantity of water or vegetable broth to modify the thickness of the puree.

Return the purée to the saucepan (if using a blender) and set it over low heat. Stir vigorously to cook the purée thoroughly.

Taste the creamy rice and cauliflower puree and adjust the spice if required.

Simmer the puree for a further 5 minutes to ensure it is cooked evenly.

Ladle the purée into serving dishes. If desired, sprinkle with fresh parsley for extra freshness and appearance.

Serve the creamy rice and cauliflower puree hot and relish its silky texture and nutritional characteristics.

Prep Time: Approximately 10 minutes

Cooking Time: Approximately 30 minutes

Nutritional Value (per serving):

Calories: 250, Fat: 7g, Carbohydrates: 43g, Fiber: 4g, Protein: 6g

4.2 Creamy Corn and Polenta Puree

Ingredients:

2 cups fresh or frozen corn kernels

1 cup cornmeal/polenta

4 cups vegetable broth

1 cup milk (dairy or plant-based)

2 tablespoons butter (or dairy-free butter replacement)

¼ cup grated Parmesan cheese (optional, eliminate for a dairy-free variation)

Salt, to taste

Pepper, to taste

Fresh chives for garnish (optional)

Instructions:

Vegetable broth should be heated up in a pot. Add the corn kernels and simmer for about 5-7 minutes, or until the corn is soft. If using frozen corn, follow the package directions for cooking.

Using a slotted spoon, remove roughly 1 cup of the cooked corn kernels from the pot and store them aside for later use.

In the same pot, turn the heat to low and add the cornmeal or polenta. Stir well to blend with the remaining broth and corn mixture.

Cook the polenta according to the package directions, stirring periodically to prevent lumps from forming. This normally takes around 20-25 minutes for the polenta to become creamy and cooked.

Once the polenta is cooked, add the milk and butter to the pot. Stir well to integrate the ingredients and achieve a creamy consistency.

If preferred, add the grated Parmesan cheese to the pot and stir until melted and thoroughly blended.

Season the creamy corn and polenta mixture with salt and pepper to taste.

Turn off the heat and give the mixture a moment to cool slightly.

Transfer the corn and polenta mixture to a blender or use an immersion blender right in the pot. Blend the ingredients until it achieves a smooth and creamy consistency.

Return the purée to the saucepan (if using a blender) and set it over low heat. Stir vigorously to cook the purée thoroughly.

Add the saved cooked corn kernels to the puree and mix gently to integrate them, imparting texture to the puree.

Taste the creamy corn and polenta puree and adjust the seasoning if required.

Simmer the puree for a further 5 minutes to ensure it is cooked evenly.

Ladle the purée into serving dishes. If desired, garnish with fresh chives for extra freshness and appearance.

Serve the creamy corn and polenta puree hot, and enjoy its smoothness and soothing taste.

Prep Time: Approximately 10 minutes

Cooking Time: Approximately 40 minutes

Nutritional Value (per serving):

Calories: 250, Fat: 9g, Carbohydrates: 38g, Fiber: 5g, Protein: 6g

4.3 Herbed Barley and Mushroom Puree

Ingredients:

1 cup pearl barley

2 cups vegetable broth 2 teaspoons olive oil

1 onion, diced

8 ounces of sliced mushrooms and 2 chopped garlic cloves

1 teaspoon dried thyme

1 teaspoon dried rosemary

Salt, to taste

Pepper, to taste

Fresh parsley for garnish (optional)

Instructions:

Rinse the pearl barley in cold water and drain.

Vegetable broth should be heated up in a pot. Add the rinsed barley and decrease the heat to low. Cover and simmer for about 30-40 minutes, or until the barley is soft and has absorbed most of the liquid. Remove from heat and put aside.

Put some olive oil in a big pan and heat it up on a stove that's not too hot. Add the chopped onion and sauté for approximately 3-4 minutes, or until the onion turns translucent.

Add the minced garlic to the pan and sauté for an additional minute until fragrant.

Add the sliced mushrooms to the pan and cook for about 5-7 minutes, or until they have softened and lost their moisture.

Sprinkle the dried thyme and rosemary over the mushroom mixture. As desired, season the meal with salt and pepper.

Stir the ingredients thoroughly, ensuring the mushrooms are covered with herbs and spices. Cook for a further 2-3 minutes to enable the flavors to mingle together.

Remove the skillet from heat and allow the mixture to cool slightly.

Transfer the cooked barley and mushroom mixture to a blender or use an immersion blender straight into the skillet. Blend the ingredients until it achieves a smooth and creamy consistency. If required, add a tiny quantity of water or vegetable broth to modify the thickness of the puree.

Return the purée to the skillet (if using a blender) and set it over low heat. Stir vigorously to cook the purée thoroughly.

Taste the herbed barley and mushroom puree and adjust the spice if required.

Simmer the puree for a further 5 minutes to ensure it is cooked evenly.

Ladle the purée into serving dishes. If desired, sprinkle with fresh parsley for extra freshness and appearance.

Serve the herbed barley and mushroom puree hot, and relish its rich tastes and nutritional characteristics.

Prep Time: Approximately 10 minutes

Cooking Time: Approximately 50 minutes

Nutritional Value (per serving):

Calories: 250, Fat: 6g, Carbohydrates: 45g, Fiber: 8g, Protein: 6g

4.4 Creamy Oatmeal and Blueberry Puree

Ingredients:

1 cup rolled oats

2 cups water

1 cup fresh or frozen blueberries

1 cup milk (dairy or plant-based)

2 tablespoons honey or maple syrup (optional)

1 teaspoon vanilla extract

Pinch of salt

Fresh blueberries for garnish (optional)

Instructions:

Put water in a pot and heat it up until it starts bubbling and steaming. Add the rolled oats and decrease the heat to low. Simmer for about 5-7 minutes, or until the oats have absorbed most of the water and turned creamy. Stir periodically to avoid sticking.

Add the blueberries to the pot and continue cooking for an additional 2-3 minutes, or until the blueberries have softened and burst somewhat. If using frozen blueberries, add a few more minutes for them to defrost and cook.

Pour in the milk of your choice and stir well to integrate it into the oats and blueberry combination.

Add honey or maple syrup, if preferred, for added sweetness. Stir well to mix.

Stir in the vanilla essence and a dash of salt. Mix thoroughly to improve the taste.

Take the pot off the stove and let the stuff inside get a little bit cooler.

Transfer the oats and blueberry mixture to a blender or use an immersion blender straight into the pot. Blend the ingredients until it achieves a smooth and creamy consistency.

Return the purée to the saucepan (if using a blender) and set it over low heat. Stir vigorously to cook the purée thoroughly.

Taste the creamy oats and blueberry puree and adjust the sweetness or saltiness as required.

Simmer the puree for a further 5 minutes to ensure it is cooked evenly.

Ladle the purée into serving dishes. If desired, garnish with fresh blueberries for enhanced freshness and appearance.

Serve the creamy oatmeal and blueberry puree warm and experience its silky texture and exquisite taste.

Prep Time: Approximately 5 minutes

Cooking Time: Approximately 15 minutes

Nutritional Value (per serving):

Calories: 250, Fat: 4g, Carbohydrates: 48g, Fiber: 6g, Protein: 6g

4.5 Quinoa and Vegetable Pilaf

Ingredients:

1 cup quinoa

Two cups vegetable broth one tablespoon olive oil

1 onion, diced

2 cloves garlic, minced

One carrot, diced one bell pepper, diced one zucchini, diced

1 cup frozen peas

1 teaspoon dried thyme

1 teaspoon ground cumin

Salt, to taste

Pepper, to taste

Fresh parsley for garnish (optional)

Instructions:

Wash the quinoa with cold water and then let the water drain out.

The vegetable broth should be cooked up in a saucepan. Add the rinsed quinoa and decrease the heat to low. Cover and simmer for about 15-20 minutes, or until the quinoa is cooked and has absorbed most of the liquid. Remove from heat and put aside.

We need to put olive oil in a big pan and heat it up on the stove at a medium temperature. Add the chopped onion and sauté for approximately 3-4 minutes, or until the onion turns translucent.

Add the minced garlic to the pan and sauté for an additional minute until fragrant.

Add the chopped carrot, bell pepper, and zucchini to the skillet. Sauté for around 5-7 minutes, or until the veggies have softened somewhat.

Stir in the frozen peas and simmer for a further 2-3 minutes, or until the peas are cooked through.

Sprinkle the dried thyme and ground cumin over the vegetable mixture. Put a little bit of salt and black dots (pepper) on your food to make it taste better.

Stir the ingredients thoroughly, ensuring the veggies are covered with the herbs and spices. Cook for a further 2-3 minutes to enable the flavors to mingle together.

Put the cooked quinoa in the pan with the vegetables. Stir gently to blend the quinoa and veggies, ensuring they are thoroughly combined.

Taste the quinoa and veggie pilaf and adjust the spice if required.

Simmer the pilaf for a further 5 minutes to ensure it is cooked evenly.

Remove the skillet from heat and allow the pilaf to cool slightly.

Serve the quinoa and veggie pilaf in a serving dish. If desired, sprinkle with fresh parsley for extra freshness and appearance.

Enjoy the quinoa and veggie pilaf as a wholesome and delectable supper.

Prep Time: Approximately 10 minutes

Cooking Time: Approximately 30 minutes

Nutritional Value (per serving):

Calories: 250, Fat: 6g, Carbohydrates: 42g, Fiber: 7g, Protein: 8g

4.6 Buckwheat and Roasted Vegetable Puree

Ingredients:

1 cup buckwheat groats

Two cups vegetable broth one tablespoon olive oil

1 onion, diced 2 cloves garlic, minced 1 carrot, diced 1 bell pepper, diced 1 zucchini, diced

1 cup cherry tomatoes

1 teaspoon dried thyme

1 teaspoon smoked paprika

Salt, to taste

Pepper, to taste

Fresh parsley for garnish (optional)

Instructions:

Drain the buckwheat groats after rinsing them in cold water.

The vegetable broth should be cooked up in a saucepan. Add the rinsed buckwheat groats and decrease the heat to low. Cover and simmer for about 15-20 minutes, or until the buckwheat is soft and has absorbed most of the liquid. Remove from heat and put aside.

Preheat the oven to 400°F (200°C).

In a large baking dish, add the chopped onion, minced garlic, carrot, bell pepper, zucchini, and cherry tomatoes.

Drizzle with olive oil and sprinkle with dried thyme, smoked paprika, salt, and pepper. Toss the veggies to coat them evenly with the spice.

Place the baking dish in the preheated oven and roast the veggies for about 20-25 minutes, or until they are soft and slightly browned. Stir the veggies halfway during the cooking time to achieve even roasting.

Remove the baking dish from the oven and allow the roasted veggies cool slightly.

Transfer the cooked buckwheat and roasted veggies to a blender or use an immersion blender straight into the baking dish. Blend the ingredients until it achieves a smooth and creamy consistency. If required, add a tiny quantity of water or vegetable broth to modify the thickness of the puree.

Return the purée to the saucepan (if using a blender) and set it over low heat. Stir vigorously to cook the purée thoroughly.

Taste the buckwheat and roasted vegetable puree and adjust the spices if required.

Simmer the puree for a further 5 minutes to ensure it is cooked evenly.

Ladle the purée into serving dishes. If desired, sprinkle with fresh parsley for extra freshness and appearance.

Serve the buckwheat and roasted vegetable puree hot, and relish its nutty tastes and healthy properties.

Prep Time: Approximately 10 minutes

Cooking Time: Approximately 45 minutes

Nutritional Value (per serving):

Calories: 250, Fat: 6g, Carbohydrates: 45g, Fiber: 8g, Protein: 7g

4.7 Creamy Pasta Alfredo

Ingredients:

8 ounces fettuccine pasta

2 tablespoons butter

2 cloves garlic, minced

1 cup heavy cream

1 cup grated Parmesan cheese

Salt, to taste

Pepper, to taste

Fresh parsley for garnish (optional)

Instructions:

Cook the fettuccine pasta until al dente according to package specifications. Set aside after draining.

Put some butter in a big pan and heat it up on the stove. Add the minced garlic and sauté for approximately 1 minute, or until fragrant.

Pour the heavy cream into the pan and bring it to a medium boil. Allow the cream to cook through for approximately 2-3 minutes, stirring regularly.

Gradually whisk in the grated Parmesan cheese, whisking continually until the sauce becomes smooth and thickens slightly.

Put a little bit of salt and pepper in the sauce until it tastes just right. Be careful with the salt since the Parmesan cheese already lends a salty taste.

Add the cooked fettuccine pasta to the pan and toss gently to coat the pasta with the creamy Alfredo sauce. Continue tossing until the pasta is completely covered and cooked through.

Taste the Creamy Pasta Alfredo and adjust the seasoning if required.

Remove the pan from heat and let the pasta remain for a minute to enable the sauce to thicken more.

Transfer the Creamy Pasta Alfredo to serving dishes or a big platter. If desired, sprinkle with fresh parsley for extra freshness and appearance.

Serve the Creamy Pasta Alfredo immediately while it is hot and enjoy the luscious and velvety texture of this traditional meal.

Prep Time: Approximately 5 minutes

Cooking Time: Approximately 15 minutes

Nutritional Value (per serving):

Calories: 550, Fat: 33g, Carbohydrates: 47g, Fiber: 2g, Protein: 18g

Chapter 5: Soups and Stews

5.1 Creamy Tomato Basil Soup

Ingredients:

2 tablespoons olive oil

1 onion, diced

2 cloves garlic, minced

4 cups ripe tomatoes, chopped

1 cup veggie broth 1 cup heavy cream

1/4 cup fresh basil leaves, chopped

Salt, to taste

Pepper, to taste

Grated Parmesan cheese for garnish (optional)

Fresh basil leaves for garnish (optional)

Instructions:

Put some olive oil in a big pot and cook it on medium heat. Add the chopped onion and minced garlic, and sauté for approximately 3-4 minutes, or until the onion turns translucent.

Add the diced tomatoes to the saucepan and simmer for a further 5 minutes, or until the tomatoes start to break down and release their juices.

Bring the mixture to a boil with the vegetarian broth. Allow it to simmer for approximately 10 minutes, or until the tomatoes are soft and tender.

Using an immersion blender or a conventional blender, slowly puree the tomato mixture until smooth and creamy.

Return the pureed soup to the pot and set it over low heat. Add the heavy cream and chopped basil leaves after that. Simmer for another 5 minutes to enable the flavors to mingle together.

Add some salt and pepper to the soup until it tastes just right. Adjust the seasoning according to your desire.

Remove the saucepan from heat and allow the Creamy Tomato Basil Soup cool slightly.

Ladle the soup into serving dishes. If preferred, top with grated Parmesan cheese and fresh basil leaves for extra taste and appearance.

Serve the Creamy Tomato Basil Soup while it is still warm, and enjoy the cozy and fragrant taste.

Prep Time: Approximately 10 minutes

Cooking Time: Approximately 25 minutes

Nutritional Value (per serving):

Calories: 280, Fat: 22g, Carbohydrates: 18g, Fiber: 3g, Protein: 5g

5.2 Hearty Chicken Noodle Soup

Ingredients:

1 tablespoon olive oil

1 onion, diced 2 carrots, sliced 2 celery stalks, sliced 2 cloves garlic, minced

8 cups chicken broth

2 cups cooked chicken, shredded

2 cups egg noodles

1 teaspoon dried thyme

1 teaspoon dried parsley

Salt, to taste

Pepper, to taste

Fresh parsley for garnish (optional)

Instructions:

Put some olive oil in a big pot and cook it on medium heat. Add the chopped onion, sliced carrots, sliced celery, and minced garlic. Sauté for approximately 5 minutes, or until the veggies begin to soften.

Add the chicken broth and make it really hot by boiling it. .Reduce the heat to low and let it simmer for approximately 10 minutes to enable the flavors to emerge.

Add the shredded cooked chicken, egg noodles, dried thyme, and dry parsley to the saucepan. Simmer for another 8-10 minutes, or until the noodles are soft and cooked through.

Add some salt and pepper to the soup until it tastes just right. Adjust the seasoning according to your desire.

Remove the saucepan from heat and allow the Hearty Chicken Noodle Soup cool slightly.

Ladle the soup into serving dishes. If desired, sprinkle with fresh parsley for extra freshness and appearance.

Serve the Hearty Chicken Noodle Soup while it is still hot, and experience the soothing tastes and healthy ingredients.

Prep Time: Approximately 10 minutes

Cooking Time: Approximately 25 minutes

Nutritional Value (per serving):

Calories: 250, Fat: 8g, Carbohydrates: 25g, Fiber: 3g, Protein: 18g

5.3 Creamy Broccoli and Cheese Soup

Ingredients:

2 tablespoons butter

1 onion, finely chopped

2 cloves garlic, minced

4 cups fresh broccoli florets

4 cups vegetable or chicken broth 1 cup heavy cream

2 cups shredded cheddar cheese

Salt and pepper to taste

Instructions:

Put butter in a big pot and heat it up on the stove. Add the chopped onion and minced garlic, and sauté until the onion turns translucent and aromatic.

Add the fresh broccoli florets to the saucepan and simmer for a few minutes, stirring regularly, until they start to soften.

Put in the chicken or vegetable stock and heat it up until it starts to bubble. Reduce the heat to low and let it simmer for approximately 15 minutes, or until the broccoli is soft.

Using an immersion blender or a conventional blender, slowly purée the soup until smooth and creamy.

Return the saucepan to low heat and mix in the heavy cream and grated cheddar cheese. Continue stirring until the cheese is melted and the soup is creamy and thoroughly blended. Add a little bit of salt and pepper until it tastes just right.

Allow the soup to boil for a further 5 minutes to mix the flavors together.

Remove from heat and serve hot. Garnish with more shredded cheese or a sprinkling of chopped fresh parsley if preferred.

Prep Time: Approximately 15 minutes

Cook Time: Approximately 30 minutes

Total Time: Approximately 45 minutes

Nutritional Value (per serving):

Calories: 320, Fat: 26g, Saturated Fat: 16g, Cholesterol: 86mg, Sodium: 600mg, Carbohydrates: 11g, Fiber: 3g, Sugar: 4g, Protein: 12g

5.4 Moroccan Spiced Vegetable Stew

Ingredients:

2 tablespoons olive oil

1 onion, diced 2 cloves garlic, minced 2 carrots, diced 2 zucchinis, diced 1 red bell pepper, diced 1 can (14 ounces) chopped tomatoes

2 cups vegetable broth

1 teaspoon ground cumin

1 teaspoon paprika

1/2 teaspoon ground cinnamon

Salt, to taste

Pepper, to taste

Fresh cilantro or parsley for garnish (optional)

Instructions:

Put some olive oil in a big pot and cook it on medium heat. Add the chopped onion and minced garlic, and sauté for approximately 3-4 minutes, or until the onion turns translucent.

Add the chopped carrots, zucchini, and red bell pepper to the saucepan. Stir and simmer for another 5 minutes, or until the veggies start to soften.

Pour in the diced tomatoes and veggie broth. Stir in the ground cumin, paprika, and ground cinnamon. Add a little bit of salt and pepper until it tastes just right.

Reduce the heat to low after the mixture has reached a boil. Cover the saucepan and let the stew simmer for approximately 20-25 minutes, or until the veggies are soft and the flavors have melted together.

Taste the Moroccan Spiced Vegetable Stew and adjust the spice if required.

Remove the saucepan from the heat and let the stew cool slightly.

Ladle the stew into serving dishes. If preferred, sprinkle with fresh cilantro or parsley for extra freshness and appearance.

Serve the Moroccan Spiced Vegetable Stew while it is still hot, and taste the fragrant spices and hearty veggies.

Prep Time: Approximately 10 minutes

Cooking Time: Approximately 35 minutes

Nutritional Value (per serving):m

Calories: 180, Fat: 7g, Carbohydrates: 27g, Fiber: 7g, Protein: 5g

5.5 Creamy Mushroom Soup

Ingredients:

1 tablespoon butter

1 tablespoon olive oil

1 onion, diced

2 cloves garlic, minced

1-pound mushrooms, sliced (such as button, cremini, or shiitake)

4 cups vegetable or chicken broth

1 cup heavy cream

1 teaspoon dried thyme

Salt, to taste

Pepper, to taste

Fresh parsley for garnish (optional)

Instructions:

In a big pot, mix the butter and olive oil together and heat them up on medium heat. Add the chopped onion and minced garlic, and sauté for approximately 3-4 minutes, or until the onion turns translucent.

Add the sliced mushrooms to the saucepan and simmer for approximately 8-10 minutes, or until the mushrooms have shed their moisture and turned golden brown.

Add the chicken or vegetable broth, then bring it to a boil. Let it cook for approximately 15 minutes to enable the flavors to emerge.

Using an immersion blender or a conventional blender, slowly mix the soup until smooth and creamy. Be careful while combining heated liquids.

Return the pureed soup to the pot and set it over low heat. Mix the thick cream and dried thyme together by stirring them. Simmer for an extra 5 minutes to allow the flavors to mingle together.

Add some salt and pepper to the soup until it tastes just perfect. Adjust the seasoning according to your desire.

Remove the saucepan from heat and allow the Creamy Mushroom Soup cool slightly.

Ladle the soup into serving dishes. If desired, sprinkle with fresh parsley for extra freshness and appearance.

Serve the Creamy Mushroom Soup while it is still hot, and enjoy the warm and velvety texture of this mushroom-infused delicacy.

Prep Time: Approximately 10 minutes

Cooking Time: Approximately 40 minutes

Nutritional Value (per serving):

Calories: 250, Fat: 21g, Carbohydrates: 12g, Fiber: 2g, Protein: 4g

5.6 Spiced Lentil Soup

Ingredients:

1 tablespoon olive oil

1 onion, diced

2 cloves garlic, minced 2 carrots, diced 2 celery stalks, diced 1 cup dry lentils (brown or green), washed and drained

4 cups vegetable broth

1 can (14 ounces) chopped tomatoes

1 teaspoon ground cumin

1/2 teaspoon ground turmeric

1/2 teaspoon paprika

Salt, to taste

Pepper, to taste

Fresh cilantro or parsley for garnish (optional)

Lemon wedges for serving (optional)

Instructions:

In a big saucepan, warm up the olive oil over medium heat. Add the chopped onion and minced garlic, and sauté for approximately 3-4 minutes, or until the onion turns translucent.

The pot should now include the chopped celery and carrots. Stir and simmer for another 5 minutes, or until the veggies start to soften.

Add the rinsed lentils, vegetable broth, diced tomatoes (with their juice), ground cumin, ground turmeric, and paprika to the saucepan. Stir well to mix.

Reduce the heat to low after the mixture has reached a boil. Cover the kettle and let the soup simmer for approximately 25-30 minutes, or until the lentils are soft and cooked through.

Add some salt and pepper to the soup until it tastes just perfect. Adjust the seasoning according to your desire.

Remove the saucepan from heat and allow the Spiced Lentil Soup cool slightly.

Ladle the soup into serving dishes. If preferred, sprinkle with fresh cilantro or parsley for extra freshness and appearance.

Serve the Spiced Lentil Soup while it is still hot. Squeeze fresh lemon juice over each dish for an added blast of flavor, if preferred.

Prep Time: Approximately 10 minutes

Cooking Time: Approximately 40 minutes

Nutritional Value (per serving):

Calories: 220, Fat: 4g, Carbohydrates: 36g, Fiber: 15g, Protein: 13g

5.7 Creamy Potato Leek Soup

Ingredients:

2 tablespoons butter

two leeks, thinly cut, with just the white and light green sections.

3 cloves garlic, minced 4 cups potatoes, peeled and diced

4 cups vegetable or chicken broth

1 cup heavy cream

Salt, to taste

Pepper, to taste

Fresh chives or parsley for garnish (optional)

Instructions:

The butter should be melted in a large pot over medium heat. Add the sliced leeks and minced garlic, and sauté for approximately 5 minutes, or until the leeks become tender and aromatic.

Add the diced potatoes to the saucepan and stir well to mix with the leeks.

Pour in the vegetable or chicken broth, ensuring that the potatoes are thoroughly covered. Reduce the heat to low after the mixture has reached a boil. Cover the saucepan and boil for approximately 20-25 minutes, or until the potatoes are soft and easily mashed with a fork.

Using an immersion blender or a conventional blender, slowly mix the soup until smooth and creamy. Be careful while combining heated liquids.

Return the pureed soup to the pot and set it over low heat. Stir in the heavy cream and To taste, add salt and pepper to the dish. Simmer for an extra 5 minutes to allow the flavors to mingle together.

Taste the soup and adjust the spice if required.

Remove the saucepan from heat and allow the Creamy Potato Leek Soup cool slightly.

Ladle the soup into serving dishes. If desired, garnish with fresh chives or parsley for extra freshness and appearance.

Serve the Creamy Potato Leek Soup while it is still hot, and relish the creamy texture and subtle tastes.

Prep Time: Approximately 10 minutes

Cooking Time: Approximately 40 minutes

Nutritional Value (per serving):

Calories: 320, Fat: 20g, Carbohydrates: 32g, Fiber: 4g, Protein: 5g

Chapter 6: Desserts and Treats

6.1 Chocolate Avocado Pudding

Ingredients:

2 ripe avocados, peeled and pitted

1/4 cup unsweetened cocoa powder

One-quarter cup honey or maple syrup (adjust to taste)

One-quarter cup almond milk (or any milk of your choice)

1 teaspoon vanilla extract

Pinch of salt

Fresh berries, sliced almonds, and grated coconut are optional garnishes.

Instructions:

In a blender or food processor, mix the ripe avocados, unsweetened cocoa powder, honey or maple syrup, almond milk, vanilla extract, and a sprinkle of salt.

Blend the ingredients until smooth and creamy, scraping down the sides of the blender or processor as required. If the mixture is too thick, add a little more almond milk, a spoonful at a time, until desired consistency is obtained.

Taste the pudding and adjust the sweetness if required by adding additional honey or maple syrup.

Transfer the Chocolate Avocado Pudding to serving dishes or glasses. Cover and refrigerate for at least 30 minutes to enable the pudding to cold and solidify.

Before serving, you may decorate the pudding with fresh berries, sliced almonds, or shredded coconut for extra texture and taste.

Enjoy the Chocolate Avocado Pudding as a tasty and healthier alternative to classic chocolate treats.

Prep Time: Approximately 10 minutes

Chilling Time: Approximately 30 minutes

Nutritional Value (per serving):

Calories: 200, Fat: 14g, Carbohydrates: 20g, Fiber: 7g, Protein: 3g

6.2 Vanilla Rice Pudding

Ingredients:

1 cup white rice

4 cups whole milk

1/2 cup granulated sugar 1 teaspoon vanilla essence

Pinch of salt

The ground cinnamon, for garnish (optional)

Instructions:

In a large saucepan, mix the white rice, whole milk, granulated sugar, vanilla essence, and a sprinkle of salt.

Place the saucepan over medium heat and bring the mixture to a boil, stirring regularly to avoid the rice from sticking to the bottom of the pan.

Once the mixture comes to a boil, lower the heat to medium and simmer uncovered, stirring periodically, for approximately 30-40 minutes, or until the rice is soft and the pudding has thickened to a creamy consistency.

Remove the pot from heat and allow the Vanilla Rice Pudding cool slightly. As it cools, the pudding will keep getting thicker.

Serve the Vanilla Rice Pudding warm or cold, depending on your choice. If desired, add ground cinnamon over top for an extra bit of taste and aesthetic appeal.

Enjoy the creamy and soothing Vanilla Rice Pudding as a lovely treat or snack.

Prep Time: Approximately 5 minutes

Cooking Time: Approximately 40 minutes

Nutritional Value (per serving):

Calories: 300, Fat: 5g, Carbohydrates: 58g, Fiber: 0g, Protein: 8g

6.3 Silky Banana Cream Pie

Ingredients:

For the crust:

1 ½ cups graham cracker crumbs

6 tablespoons unsalted butter, melted

2 teaspoons granulated sugar

For the filling:

1 ½ cups ripe bananas, mashed (approximately 3 medium bananas)

½ cup granulated sugar

¼ cup cornstarch ¼ teaspoon salt

4 big egg yolks

2 cups whole milk

2 tablespoons unsalted butter

1 teaspoon vanilla extract

For the topping:

1 cup heavy cream

2 teaspoons powdered sugar

Sliced bananas, for garnish

Instructions:

Preheat the oven to 350°F (175°C).

For the crust, combine the crushed graham crackers, melted butter, and granulated sugar in a mixing dish. Just enough stirring will make the mixture resemble wet sand.

Press the crumb mixture evenly over the bottom and up the edges of a 9-inch pie plate. Use the back of a spoon or a flat-bottomed glass to firmly push the crust into place.

The crust should bake for 10 minutes, or until golden brown, in the preheated oven. Remove from the oven and put aside to cool fully.

In a saucepan, mix together the mashed bananas, granulated sugar, cornstarch, salt, egg yolks, and milk for the filling. Place the saucepan over medium heat and simmer, stirring regularly, until the mixture thickens and comes to a mild boil.

Remove the pot from heat and mix in the butter and vanilla extract until well-integrated. Allow the filling to cool for a short while.

Pour the banana filling into the chilled crust and distribute it evenly. Cover the pie with plastic wrap, ensuring the cover contacts the surface of the filling to prevent skin from developing. Chill the pie in the refrigerator for at least 4 hours, or until totally set.

Just before serving, make the whipped cream topping. In a mixing bowl, beat the heavy cream and powdered sugar until soft peaks form.

Spread the whipped cream over the cold pie filling, covering it thoroughly. Garnish with sliced bananas for an added sense of freshness and appearance.

Slice and serve the Silky Banana Cream Pie, appreciating each mouthful of its silky texture and exquisite taste.

Prep Time: Approximately 30 minutes

Chilling Time: Approximately 4 hours

Nutritional Value (per serving):

Calories: 420, Fat: 25g, Carbohydrates: 46g, Fiber: 2g, Protein: 5g

6.4 Creamy Pumpkin Pie Puree

Ingredients:

2 cups pumpkin puree

1 cup heavy cream

1/2 cup brown sugar 2 big eggs

One teaspoon of vanilla extract 1 teaspoon of cinnamon powder

1/2 teaspoon ground ginger

1/4 teaspoon ground nutmeg

1/4 teaspoon ground cloves

Pinch of salt

Instructions:

Preheat the oven to 350°F (175°C).

In a large mixing bowl, add the pumpkin puree, heavy cream, brown sugar, eggs, vanilla essence, ground cinnamon, ground ginger, ground nutmeg, ground cloves, and a touch of salt. Whisk together until fully integrated and smooth.

Pour the pumpkin mixture into a baking dish or individual ramekins, ensuring it is evenly spread.

Place the baking dish or ramekins in the preheated oven and bake for approximately 30-35 minutes, or until the puree is set and a toothpick inserted into the middle comes out clean.

Remove the Creamy Pumpkin Pie Puree from the oven and allow it cool to room temperature.

Once cooled, cover the dish or ramekins with plastic wrap and refrigerate for at least 2 hours, or until totally cold and set.

Serve the Creamy Pumpkin Pie Puree as a lovely dessert, either on its own or topped with a dollop of whipped cream and a sprinkling of cinnamon.

Prep Time: Approximately 10 minutes

Baking Time: Approximately 30-35 minutes

Chilling Time: Approximately 2 hours

Nutritional Value (per serving):

Calories: 220, Fat: 13g, Carbohydrates: 24g, Fiber: 3g, Protein: 4g

6.5 Cinnamon Apple Crumble

Ingredients:

For the apple filling:

4 cups apples, peeled, cored, and sliced

1/4 cup granulated sugar

2 tablespoons all-purpose flour

1 teaspoon ground cinnamon

1/4 teaspoon ground nutmeg

1 tablespoon lemon juice

For the crumble topping:

1 cup all-purpose flour

1/2 cup granulated sugar

1/2 cup unsalted butter, chilled and chopped into tiny pieces

1/2 teaspoon ground cinnamon

Pinch of salt

Instructions:

Preheat the oven to 375°F (190°C).

In a large bowl, mix the sliced apples, granulated sugar, all-purpose flour, ground cinnamon, ground nutmeg, and lemon juice. Toss the mixture until the apples are uniformly covered.

Transfer the apple filling onto a baking dish, spreading it out evenly.

In a separate dish, make the crumble topping. Combine the all-purpose flour, granulated sugar, cold unsalted butter pieces, ground cinnamon, and a pinch of salt. Use your fingers or a pastry cutter to combine the ingredients until the crumbs and the butter are uniformly spread.

Sprinkle the crumble topping over the apple filling, covering it thoroughly.

Place the baking dish in the preheated oven and bake for approximately 30-35 minutes, or until the apples are soft and the crumble topping is golden brown and crunchy.

Remove the Cinnamon Apple Crumble from the oven and allow it cool for a few minutes before serving.

Serve the Cinnamon Apple Crumble warm, either on its own or with a scoop of vanilla ice cream or a dollop of whipped cream.

Prep Time: Approximately 15 minutes

Baking Time: Approximately 30-35 minutes

Nutritional Value (per serving):

Calories: 250, Fat: 11g, Carbohydrates: 38g, Fiber: 3g, Protein: 2g

6.6 Berry and Yogurt Parfait

Ingredients:

One cup mixed berry (like strawberries, blueberries, or raspberries)

1 cup plain or flavored yogurt (Greek yogurt or normal yogurt)

1/4 cup granola or muesli

Honey or maple syrup, for drizzling (optional)

Fresh mint leaves, for garnish (optional)

Instructions:

Wash and prepare the mixed berries by slicing the strawberries and removing any stems. If using frozen berries, defrost them according to the package directions.

In a glass or a parfait dish, begin stacking the ingredients. Start with a dollop of yogurt at the bottom of the glass, followed by a layer of mixed berries.

Repeat the layers until all the ingredients are utilized, finishing with a layer of yogurt on top.

Sprinkle the granola or muesli equally over the yogurt layer, providing a delightful crunch to the parfait.

Drizzle honey or maple syrup over the top if preferred, providing a touch of sweetness.

Garnish with fresh mint leaves for an added burst of freshness and presentation.

Serve the Berry and Yogurt Parfait immediately or refrigerate for a bit to cool and allow the flavors to melt together.

Use a spoon to scoop between the layers, savoring the mix of creamy yogurt, luscious berries, and crunchy granola.

Prep Time: Approximately 10 minutes

Nutritional Value (per serving):

Calories: 200, Fat: 5g, Carbohydrates: 30g, Fiber: 4g, Protein: 10g

6.7 Chilled Watermelon Soup

Ingredients:

4 cups diced seedless watermelon

1 tablespoon freshly squeezed lime juice

1 tablespoon freshly squeezed lemon juice

1 tablespoon honey or agave syrup (optional, for extra sweetness)

1-2 sprigs of fresh mint leaves, plus additional for garnish

Pinch of salt

Fresh berries or chopped watermelon, for garnish (optional)

Instructions:

In a blender or food processor, add the cubed watermelon, lime juice, lemon juice, honey or agave syrup (if wanted), fresh mint leaves, and a touch of salt.

Blend the ingredients on high speed until smooth and fully blended. Taste the soup and adjust the sweetness or acidity by adding additional honey or citrus juice, if desired.

Once combined, transfer the soup to a closed container and refrigerate for at least 1 hour to enable the flavors to merge and the soup to cool.

Before serving, give the cold soup a vigorous stir. If it has thickened too much, you may think it out with a dash of water.

Ladle the Chilled Watermelon Soup into bowls or serving glasses.

Garnish with fresh mint leaves and, if preferred, more fresh berries or sliced watermelon for added texture and color.

Serve the Chilled Watermelon Soup immediately, enabling everyone to enjoy the refreshing taste and freshness of the soup.

Prep Time: Approximately 10 minutes

Chilling Time: Minimum 1 hour

Nutritional Value (per serving):

Calories: 60, Fat: 0g, Carbohydrates: 15g, Fiber: 1g, Protein: 1g

Manufactured by Amazon.ca
Bolton, ON

37747642R00061